LOUISIANA

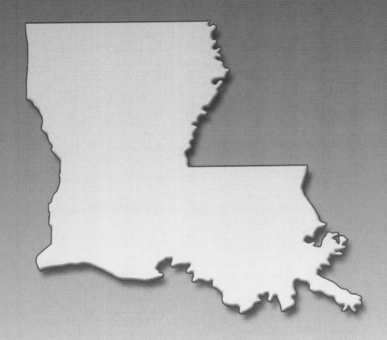

by Patricia Lantier

GARETH**STEVENS**
PUBLISHING
A Member of the WRC Media Family of Companies

Please visit our web site at: www.garethstevens.com
For a free color catalog describing Gareth Stevens Publishing's
list of high-quality books and multimedia programs, call
1-800-542-2595 (USA) or 1-800-387-3178 (Canada).
Gareth Stevens Publishing's fax: (877) 542-2596.

Library of Congress Cataloging-in-Publication Data

Lantier, Patricia, 1952-
    Louisiana / Patricia Lantier.
        p. cm. — (Portraits of the states)
    Includes bibliographical references and index.
    ISBN-10: 0-8368-4667-2   ISBN-13: 978-0-8368-4667-6 (lib. bdg.)
    ISBN-10: 0-8368-4686-9   ISBN-13: 978-0-8368-4686-7 (softcover)
    1. Louisiana—Juvenile literature. I. Title. II. Series.
    F369.3L36   2006
    976.3—dc22   2005044477

Updated edition reprinted in 2007. First published in 2006 by
Gareth Stevens Publishing
A Weekly Reader Company
1 Reader's Digest Rd.
Pleasantville, NY 10570-7000 USA

Editorial direction: Mark J. Sachner
Project manager: Jonatha A. Brown
Editor: Catherine Gardner
Art direction and design: Tammy West
Picture research: Diane Laska-Swanke
Indexer: Walter Kronenberg
Production: Jessica Morris and Robert Kraus

Picture credits: Cover, pp. 9, 26, 27, 28 © Philip Gould; pp. 4, 20, 21, 22, 24
© John Elk III; p. 5 © PhotoDisc; p. 6 © ArtToday; p. 8 © Library of Congress;
p. 10 © MPI/Getty Images; pp. 12, 17 Jocelyn Augustino/FEMA; p. 15 © Joseph
Scherschel/Time & Life Pictures/Getty Images; pp. 16, 25 © Gibson Stock
Photography; p. 29 © Ronald Martinez/Getty Images

Printed in the United States of America

2 3 4 5 6 7 8 9 10 09 08 07

CONTENTS

★ ★

Words that are defined in the Glossary appear
in **bold** the first time they are used in the text.

On the Cover: Rex has been King of the Mardi Gras Carnival in New
Orleans since 1872. The Rex parade is huge, with many colorful floats

Introduction

If you could visit Louisiana, what would you like to see? A Mardi Gras parade? Native ruins at Poverty Point? Alligators swimming in dark **bayous**? Louisiana is a great place to visit.

The state has **swamps**, giant oaks, bayous, and green forests. It has long, steamy summers and short, mild winters. It also has music, mystery, and delicious food.

The people of Louisiana are warm and friendly. They are proud of their history and way of life. They enjoy showing visitors how to "pass a good time."

Welcome to Louisiana!

The Atchafalaya Basin in Louisiana covers almost 600,000 acres (242,800 hectares) of swampland. It is a valuable wilderness of plant and animal life.

The state flag of Louisiana.

LOUISIANA FACTS

- Became the 18th U.S. State: April 30, 1812
- Population (2006): 4,287,768
- Capital: Baton Rouge
- Biggest Cities: New Orleans, Baton Rouge, Shreveport, Lafayette
- Size: 43,562 square miles (112,826 square kilometers)
- Nickname: The Pelican State
- State Tree: Bald cypress
- State Flower: Magnolia
- State Mammal: Black bear
- State Bird: Eastern brown pelican

History

Native Americans have lived in Louisiana for thousands of years. One early group lived in an area now called Poverty Point. These Natives built giant **mounds** out of earth and clay. Their homes were made of mud and grass.

Explorers and Settlers

Spanish explorers visited the region as early as 1519. But Robert de La Salle claimed the land for France in 1682. He named it *Louisiana*. He chose this name to honor Louis XIV, the king of France. The first French settlement was Fort St. Jean Baptiste. It was founded in 1714.

A Scotsman named John Law brought new settlers into the area. He brought slaves from Africa, too. Rich planters

Robert de La Salle claimed Louisiana for France. He marked the area with a large cross and a column that was carved with the French king's coat of arms.

Pirate and Patriot

Jean Lafitte was a famous pirate. He sailed the waters of the Gulf of Mexico. He and his crew attacked other ships. They stole goods to sell in New Orleans. Lafitte hid on islands along the Louisiana coast. During the War of 1812, the British tried to hire Lafitte. But he wanted to fight for the United States. He and his pirate crew fought in the Battle of New Orleans.

bought the slaves to work on huge farms called **plantations**. In 1718, Law asked Jean Baptiste Le Moyne, Sieur de Bienville, to start a new town. They named it New Orleans.

A group of Acadians arrived in the 1750s. They came from Canada. They had their own way of life and spoke French. They left their homes after Britain took the area from France.

Many settled in South Louisiana. The Acadians later became known as "Cajuns" (KAY-juns).

In 1762, France gave all its land west of the Mississippi River to Spain. Spain gave the land back to France in 1800. The United States bought the land from France in 1803. This large region was known as the Louisiana Purchase.

Territory and Statehood

The Louisiana Purchase was

Mossy Trees

Live oak trees grow throughout Louisiana. They can live to be very old. Spanish moss often hangs from the tree limbs. This stringy gray plant was used in the past to stuff mattresses.

FUN FACTS

Bird Story

Louisiana is the Pelican State. The brown pelican is the state emblem. This bird dives into the water to fill its large beak with food and water. The water filters out, and the food remains. Some stories say if food is hard to find, the parent birds will tear off pieces of their bodies to feed their babies.

This French map is from the 1750s. It shows the Mississippi River dividing America, including the Louisiana Territory, into two parts.

a huge area of land. Part of this land later became the state of Louisiana. At first, it was named the **Territory of Orleans.**

Louisiana became a state in 1812. The War of 1812 began the same year. One of the major battles of the war was the Battle of New Orleans. It took place on January 8, 1815. There were twice as many British soldiers as U.S soldiers. Even so, the U.S. troops won.

Civil War

The U.S. states did not agree on the issue of slavery. This issue tore the country in two. Southern states wanted to keep slavery. They broke away and

broke away and formed their own country. They named it the Confederate States of America. Northern states wanted to end slavery and keep the country together.

The Civil War began in 1861. It lasted four years. Louisiana fought for the South. Both the North and the South wanted to control New Orleans. The city was important because of its location at the mouth of the Mississippi River. Union, or U.S.,

This is the tomb of famous voodoo priestess Marie Laveau. It is in St. Louis Cemetery No. I in New Orleans.

IN LOUISIANA'S HISTORY

Voodoo Queen

Voodoo is a religion that began in Africa. Slaves brought it to America. People who practice voodoo ask spirits to make their wishes come true. One voodoo **priestess** was Marie Laveau. She lived in New Orleans in the 1800s. People asked her to help them with their problems. She became famous. Since her death, people have visited her tomb. They still ask for her help and leave gifts, messages, and money.

troops captured New Orleans in 1862. The North won the war, and slavery came to an end. Louisiana became part of the Union again. But the war had ruined the state.

After the war, U.S. soldiers stayed in the South to help rebuild the area. They also wanted to see that former slaves had equal rights. The soldiers stayed in Louisiana longer than in any other state.

The people of Louisiana had to start over. Their way of life was gone. Many went back to farming. Oil and natural gas became important. **Factories** were built to make new products.

IN LOUISIANA'S HISTORY

Special Service by Black Soldiers
When Union troops captured New Orleans, many black men joined the Union Army. Most of these men were slaves. A few of them were free blacks who owned their own homes. All of them wanted to fight for freedom. They were the first and largest black regiment in the Union Army.

The Battle of Port Hudson was fought in 1863 during the Civil War. The Union won the battle.

A New Century

World War I and World War II were fought overseas during the first half of the twentieth century. Soldiers from Louisiana and all the other states fought in these wars. During and after World War II, the number of factories in Louisiana grew by about 60 percent.

Huey P. Long was governor at the start of the **Great Depression** in the 1930s. This difficult time began in the early 1930s. The prices people paid for goods fell. Workers lost their jobs.

Equality

Slaves were free after the Civil War. But most African Americans in the state did not have equal rights. In the 1950s, this began to change. Black and white children

Famous People of Louisiana

Huey Pierce Long

Born: August 30, 1893, Winnfield, Louisiana

Died: September 10, 1935, Baton Rouge, Louisiana

Huey P. Long was governor of Louisiana from 1928 to 1932. He began as a poor farm boy. He taught himself the law and got a degree. Long believed rich people should share their money with the poor. He built new roads, bridges, and hospitals. He also improved the state school system. Long was so powerful he called himself the "Kingfish." He was shot and killed in the state capitol in 1935.

finally were allowed to go to the same schools in 1960. Ernest Morial became the first black mayor of New Orleans in 1977. Today, the

Hurricane Katrina destroyed much of southeastern Louisiana. This photo shows an entire area of homes that were completely flooded.

law gives equal rights to people of all races.

Katrina!

In August 2005, **Hurricane** Katrina hit Louisiana. Winds swept through New Orleans at 125 miles (201 km) per hour. Buildings were destroyed. Most of the city was under water. The damage was terrible. People lost their homes and pets. Many lost their lives. Only a few weeks later, another huge storm, Hurricane Rita, hit. It too caused a great amount of damage.

IN LOUISIANA'S HISTORY

Port of New Orleans

New Orleans is located at the mouth of the Mississippi River. Its port has long been important for trade. In the past, boats from many places docked in New Orleans to buy and sell goods. Steamboats began traveling up and down the river in 1812. They carried both goods and passengers. Steamboats still take tourists along the coast. Larger ships and tankers have replaced the steamboats for transporting goods.

1500s	Spanish explorers visit the Louisiana region.
1682	French explorer Robert de La Salle claims the Mississippi River Valley for France.
1714	The first European settlement in Louisiana is founded at Fort St. Jean Baptiste.
mid 1700s	French-speaking Acadians from eastern Canada settle in southern Louisiana. They later become known as "Cajuns."
1803	The United States buys Louisiana from France in a huge land sale called the Louisiana Purchase.
1812	Louisiana becomes the eighteenth U.S. state.
1812–1815	The War of 1812 is fought between the U.S. and Britain.
1861–1865	The North fights the South in the Civil War. More than twenty major battles are fought in Louisiana.
1917–1918	Soldiers from Louisiana fight in World War I.
1941–1945	Louisiana sends soldiers to fight in World War II.
1977	Ernest Morial is elected as first African-American mayor of New Orleans.
1997	Mary Landrieu is elected as Louisiana's first female U.S. senator.
2003	Kathleen Babineaux Blanco is elected as first female governor of Louisiana.
2005	Hurricane Katrina strikes the Gulf Coast, causing great damage to the New Orleans area of Louisiana. It destroys parts of Mississippi and Alabama, as well. Hurricane Rita hits less than one month later.

People

Louisiana is home to more than four million people. Native Americans were the first to live there. When white settlers came, many Natives moved to the swamps and **prairies**. Several tribes were able to survive. About twenty-five thousand Natives live in the state today. Many still speak their own language and practice Native ways.

Acadians, or "Cajuns," live in the southern part of the state. Many Cajuns speak a mix of English and French.

Hispanics: In the 2000 U.S. Census, 2.4 percent of the people in the state of Louisiana called themselves Latino or Hispanic. Most of them or their relatives came from places where Spanish is spoken. They may come from different racial backgrounds.

The People of Louisiana

Total Population 4,287,768

White
63.9%

Native American
0.6%

Asian
1.2%

Other
1.8%

Black or African American
32.5%

Percentages are based on the 2000 Census.

This photograph of Cajun children was taken in the 1940s. The children lived in Marksville, which is in the east-central part of the state.

Creoles also live mostly in the southern part of the state. Their families go back to the first French and Spanish settlers in the area. People from other countries moved to the state in the 1800s. They blended into the Creole culture.

African Americans first came to the state as slaves or as free people of color. Today, this group forms more than 30 percent of the state's **population**.

More than two-thirds of the people in the state live in or near large cities. New Orleans is the state's largest city. It often is called "The Big Easy." The way of life seems fun and relaxed. Two out of three people in the city are African Americans. People whose families once came from Europe make up the second-largest group in New Orleans.

The city of New Orleans rises up from the banks of the Mississippi River. This evening photo was taken from across the river.

Education

The first schools in the state were private schools. They were run by priests. Public schools first opened in 1808. Today, more than 879,000 students in the state attend public and private schools.

Louisiana has strong colleges and universities. Some are public. Some are private. Louisiana State in Baton Rouge is the largest. It has courses in every parish in the state. Tulane and Loyola in New Orleans are excellent private universities.

Religion

More than 94 percent of the

people in Louisiana today are Christians. About 35 percent of them are Roman Catholics. Nearly 30 percent are Baptists. About 5 percent are Methodists. Smaller numbers of people practice other religions.

After Hurricane Katrina struck New Orleans, many people were left stranded. Everyone who could help worked together to rescue people and provide relief.

Famous People of Louisiana

Jimmie Davis

Born: September 11, 1899, Quitman, Louisiana

Died: November 5, 2000, Baton Rouge, Louisiana

James Houston Davis had ten brothers and sisters. His family was poor. They all lived in a two-bedroom house. His parents believed in education even though they did not have a lot of money. Davis went to school. He worked his way through college. He also sang and played the guitar. His most famous song was "You Are My Sunshine." It became one of Louisiana's state songs. Davis was elected governor of the state in 1944 and again in 1960.

The Land

Louisiana has three main regions. The West Gulf Coastal Plain covers the western part of the state. The flat plains in this area slope toward the Gulf of Mexico. The coast has sandy beaches. The area also has marshes that contain salt domes. The northern part of this area has rolling hills.

The Mississippi Alluvial Plain surrounds the Mississippi River. The river flows through the state to the Gulf of Mexico. **Silt** that is rich in minerals flows with the water. The silt collects at the mouth of the river. This forms a **delta**. The delta grows in size as more silt is deposited. The river water flows in and around the delta to reach the Gulf. The soil in this area is very fertile because of the silt.

The East Gulf Coastal Plain lies north of the city of New Orleans and Lake Pontchartrain. It is a land of marshes and grass.

The highest point in the state is Driskill Mountain. It rises 535 feet (163 meters) above sea level.

FUN FACTS

Salty Secret

A small sea once covered the area that is now Louisiana. As the climate changed, the sea dried up. It left behind huge deposits of salt. This salt soon was covered with soil. After thousands of years, the salt and soil began to push upward. This formed big mounds and hills called salt domes. The state has many of these domes. People mine the salt in the domes.

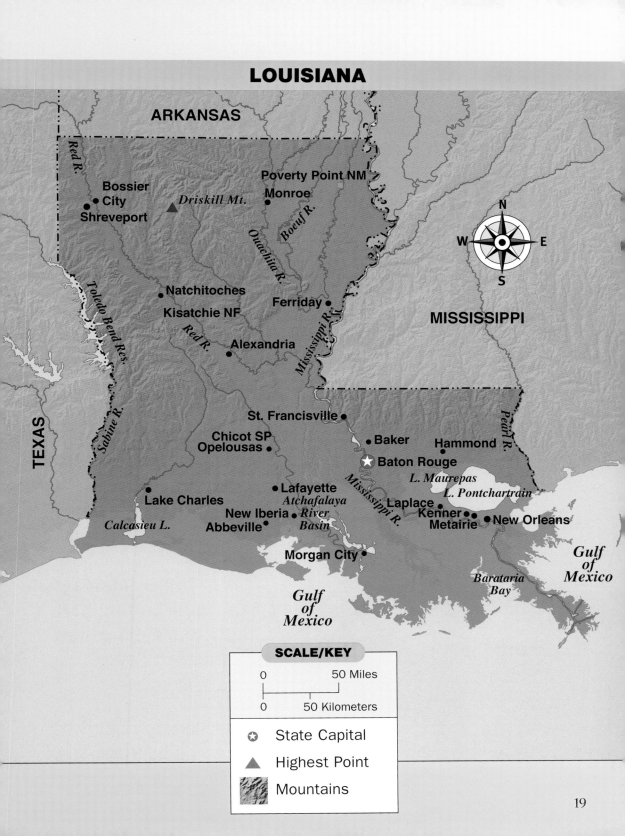

LOUISIANA

ARKANSAS

Red R.

Bossier City
Shreveport

▲ *Driskill Mt.*

Poverty Point NM
Monroe

Boeuf R.

Ouachita R.

Natchitoches

Kisatchie NF

Ferriday

Red R.

Alexandria

Toledo Bend Res.

Sabine R.

TEXAS

Mississippi R.

MISSISSIPPI

N
W   E
S

St. Francisville

Chicot SP
Opelousas

Baker

Hammond

★ Baton Rouge

Pearl R.

L. Maurepas

L. Pontchartrain

Lake Charles

Lafayette
Atchafalaya
River
Basin

New Iberia
Abbeville

Calcasieu L.

Mississippi R.

Laplace
Kenner
Metairie

New Orleans

Morgan City

Gulf of Mexico

Barataria Bay

Gulf of Mexico

SCALE/KEY

0 ———————— 50 Miles

0 ———————— 50 Kilometers

⊛ State Capital

▲ Highest Point

▦ Mountains

FACTS

Oak Alley

Before the Civil War, many plantations were built along rivers in Louisiana. While slaves worked hard in the fields, the owners lived in large homes. Oak Alley Plantation was built in 1839. It is one of the most beautiful homes from that time left today. A long driveway lined with giant oak trees leads to the front of the home. The trees are three hundred years old.

Major Rivers

Mississippi River
2,357 miles (3,792 km) long

Red River
1,018 miles (1,638 km) long

Ouachita River
605 miles (974 km) long

Climate

The state has a warm, humid climate. Summers are long, hot, and steamy. Winters are short and mild. Louisiana receives about 60 inches (1,524 millimeters) of rain a year. More rain falls in July than in the other months. Snow rarely falls. In late summer and early autumn, hurricanes sometimes strike the coast.

Waterways

The state has many rivers. The Mississippi River is the longest.

Oak Alley Plantation was built by Jacques T. Roman. Twenty-eight huge oak trees line the entrance alley.

The southern region has small streams called bayous (BUY-yous). The state has low land, and many of the rivers overflow their banks. Water then floods the land. People have lost farms and homes to floods. The city of New Orleans is below sea level. In many places, concrete walls and high earth walls called "levees" (LEV-eez) are built to protect against flooding. But Hurricane Katrina was a very strong storm. Some of the walls broke, and water rushed into the city.

Plants and Animals

Nearly half of Louisiana is forest. About 150 types of trees grow in these forests. Wildflowers and shrubs also grow in the state.

Alligators and snakes live in swamps and bayous. The waterways have lots of fish, such as bass and catfish. Crawfish live in small streams and bayous. The state also has other kinds of shellfish.

Raccoons, mink, and black bears live in the swampy southern region. Gray squirrels and white-tailed deer also are common.

Many types of birds live in Louisiana. The brown pelican is the state bird. It also is an endangered species. The birds are in danger of dying out. Laws now protect these birds and their homes.

A snowy egret rests on a cypress tree limb in a Louisiana swamp. The bald cypress is the official state tree.

21

Economy

Louisiana has been a busy trading center since the French settled there. Today, the Port of South Louisiana handles more tons of goods than any other port in the country. The Louisiana Superport is 20 miles (32 km) off the state coast. It is one of the few ports deep enough for huge oil tankers.

The first natural gas in the state was found in 1823. The first oil was found in 1901. Today, oil and gas production still are growing. This means jobs for

Shrimp fishermen head out in their netted boat for a day of work. Shrimp are part of many local dishes. They also are sold worldwide.

many people. Other people work in mining and forestry.

Farming and Fishing

Farming remains important. Crops include sugarcane, sweet potatoes, cotton, and rice. Some of the land is used for **grazing** animals.

The state supplies about one-fourth of all the fish in the country. The state also has a lot of shellfish.

Tourism

People from all around the world visit Louisiana. Many want to see New Orleans. Others want to see the bayou country. Some want to see Mardi Gras (MAHR-dee GRAH). Many come to enjoy the state's natural beauty. These people spend lots of money in the state.

How Money Is Made in Louisiana

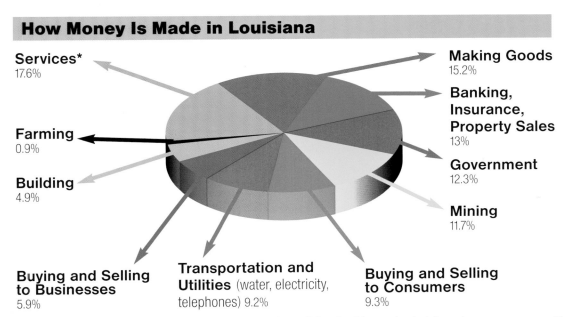

Services*
17.6%

Farming
0.9%

Building
4.9%

Making Goods
15.2%

Banking, Insurance, Property Sales
13%

Government
12.3%

Mining
11.7%

Buying and Selling to Businesses
5.9%

Transportation and Utilities (water, electricity, telephones) 9.2%

Buying and Selling to Consumers
9.3%

* Services include jobs in hotels, restaurants, auto repair, medicine, teaching, and entertainment.

Government

Baton Rouge is Louisiana's capital city. The state's lawmakers work there. The government has three parts. These parts are the executive, legislative, and judicial branches.

Executive Branch

The governor is head of the executive branch. This branch makes sure state laws are carried out. The lieutenant governor helps the governor. Other officials belong to the executive branch.

Louisiana's State Capitol in Baton Rouge was built in 1932. It was the special project of Huey P. Long, governor of the state at that time. The capitol is thirty-four stories high.

24

The Louisiana governor's mansion is in Baton Rouge. It was built in 1963. Many special events for the public are held at the mansion and on its grounds.

Legislative Branch

The legislative branch makes state laws. The **legislature** has two bodies. They are the Senate and the House of Representatives. The Senate and the House work together.

Judicial Branch

Judges and courts make up the judicial branch. Judges and courts may decide whether people who have been accused of committing crimes are guilty.

Local Government

Louisiana has sixty-four parishes. These are like the counties in other states. A team of people runs almost every parish. Each team is called a police jury.

LOUISIANA'S STATE GOVERNMENT

Executive		Legislative		Judicial	
Office	**Length of Term**	**Body**	**Length of Term**	**Court**	**Length of Term**
Governor	4 years	Senate (39 members)	4 years	Supreme (7 judges)	10 years
Lieutenant Governor	4 years	House of Representatives (105 members)	4 years	Appeals (53 judges)	10 years

Things to See and Do

The people of Louisiana enjoy working hard and having fun. One local saying is, "Let the good times roll." The state offers many ways to have a good time.

Yummy for the Tummy

The state has great food. Spicy Cajun and Creole dishes are favorites. Visitors can try lots of tasty local treats.

Mardi Gras Magic

Mardi Gras (MAR-dee GRAH) is a big party that takes place every year in New Orleans and a few other cities in the state. Mardi Gras parades have marching bands. People in costumes and masks ride

Corn on the cob, lemon slices, fat red crawfish, and secret spices — a perfectly delicious crawfish boil!

Louis Armstrong

Born: August 4, 1901, New Orleans, Louisiana

Died: July 6, 1971, New York, New York

Louis Daniel Armstrong was a famous jazz musician. He was born in New Orleans to a poor family. At fourteen, Armstrong was sent to a special school for boys. While there, he learned to play the **cornet**. Armstrong loved music and spent his life playing and singing all over the world. His wonderful sound and joyful manner made people happy.

on floats. They toss coins, beads, and candy to the crowds.

Museums

Museums help celebrate the state's history. The Louisiana Purchase was signed at the Cabildo in New Orleans. This building is now part of the Louisiana State Museum. The Old State Capitol in Baton

The Cabildo was built in New Orleans' French Quarter in 1799. The Louisiana Purchase was signed in the Cabildo.

Rouge and the Delta Music Museum in Ferriday also show life as it was in the past.

Many old plantation homes are open to visitors. Oak Alley, Houmas House, and Nottoway are just a few. The Myrtles in St. Francisville is said to be a real haunted house.

Music, Music, Everywhere

Jazz was born in New Orleans. Blues music has strong ties to the area. Cajun and Zydeco music began in the swamps and bayou lands. The state has many music festivals each year.

The Great Outdoors

The state has many parks. The largest is Chicot State Park. Rolling hills, thick forests, and a lake are good for hiking, boating, fishing, and other activities.

State and national forests offer lots of room for fun. Visitors can go camping, biking, horseback riding, and more.

New Orleans hosts the Jazz and Heritage Festival every year in spring. This ten-day festival offers music, food, and arts and crafts.

There also are swamp tours, huge **crawfish boils**, and walks along old Native trails.

Sports

The state has two big-league sports teams. The New Orleans Saints football team first played in the city in 1966. In basketball, the New Orleans Hornets have been in the city since 2002.

College sports teams have lots of fans, especially Louisiana State University in Baton Rouge. The Sugar Bowl is a major college football game. It takes place in New Orleans every New Year's Day.

Famous People of Louisiana

Anne Rice

Born: October 4, 1941, New Orleans, Louisiana

Anne Rice is a popular writer. Her birth name was Howard Allen O'Brien. She changed it to Anne as a child. She married a poet named Stan Rice when she was twenty years old. Anne Rice has written many novels that have sold all around the world. Some of the most famous are about vampires.

In this professional football game, the New Orleans Saints run the ball past the Dallas Cowboys.

★ ★

bayous — small, slow-moving rivers

cornet — a musical instrument; a type of horn

crawfish boils — giant outdoor cookouts, with huge pots of crawfish, red potatoes, corn on the cob, onions, and secret seasonings boiled together in water

delta — the silt that has built up at the mouth of a river

factories — buildings where goods and products are made

grazing — feeding on grass or crops in a field

Great Depression — a time, in the 1930s, when many people lost their jobs and businesses lost money

hurricane — a storm that brings high winds and sheets of rain

legislature — a group that makes laws

mounds — round hills made of earth or stone

plantations — very large farms that need many people to tend the crops

population — the number of people who live in a place, such as a state

prairies — large, grassy areas of land

priestess — a woman who leads a religion

silt — loose pieces of soil

swamps — wooded wetlands that are partly covered with water

territory — an area that belongs to a country

Books

Louisiana Indian Tales. Elizabeth Moore and Alice Couvillon (Pelican Publishing Company)

Louisiana Purchase. Ready-For-Chapters (series). Connie Roop and Peter Roop (Aladdin)

Mardi Gras Dictionary. Beverly B. Vidrine (Pelican Publishing)

New Orleans Saints. Julie Nelson (Creative Education)

P Is for Pelican: A Louisiana Alphabet. Discover America State by State (series). Anita Prieto (Thomson Gale)

Web Sites

Louisiana Plantations
www.eatel.net/~meme/Plantations.html

Louisiana Secretary of State: Louisiana Facts Index
www.sec.state.la.us/around/all.htm

Louisiana Department of Culture, Recreation, and Tourism
www.crt.state.la.us/parks/

Louisiana Agriculture and Forestry Fun Farm Facts
www.louisiana.gov/wps/portal/.cmd/cs/.ce/155/.s/1118/_s.155/
1088/_me/1117/ (click on Fun Farm Facts for Kids)

INDEX